Beautiful Bharat

OrangeBooks Publication

1st Floor, Rajhans Arcade, Mall Road, Kohka, Bhilai, Chhattisgarh 490020

Website: **www.orangebooks.in**

© Copyright, 2024, Author

All rights reserved. No part of this book may be reproduced, stored in a retrieval system, or transmitted, in any form by any means, electronic, mechanical, magnetic, optical, chemical, manual, photocopying, recording or otherwise, without the prior written consent of its writer.

First Edition, 2024

Beautiful Bharat

OJASVI KHANDELWAL

OrangeBooks Publication
www.orangebooks.in

Content

Seven Secrets of Success _____ vii

Poem – 1
Mother Earth _____ 1

Poem – 2
Save Water _____ 3

Poem – 3
Christmas _____ 5

Poem – 4
Flowers _____ 6

Poem – 5
Summer _____ 9

Poem – 6
Festivals _____ 10

Poem – 7
  Chandrayaan – 3 _____ 12

Poem – 8
  Wedding _____ 15

Poem – 9
  Bones _____ 16

Poem – 10
  God _____ 18

Seven Secrets of Success

1. **Roof**   = *Aim High*
2. **Fan**   = *Be Cool*
3. **Clock**   = *Every minute is precious*
4. **Window**   = *See the world*
5. **Calendar** = *Be up to date*
6. **Mirror**   = *Reflect before you act*
7. **Door**   = *Push hard to achieve your goal*

Poem – 1

Mother Earth

Mother Earth, Mother Earth,
She is the one who gave us birth.
I love the plants and the beauty it grants.
Its home for you and home for me.
Dear Earth you can depend on me.
Instead of a bike, I'll take a hike.
I'll reuse, reduce and recycle.
Instead of a car, I'll use a bicycle.
I'll grow a garden and guard it like a warden.
I'm small but I deeply care
Because it's a planet we all share
Mother Earth, Mother Earth
Make it again full of mirth.

Ojasvi Khandelwal

Poem – 2
Save Water

We don't care, we don't need,
But one day we will seek.
Dirt water all around, disease all around,
No purity, no security.
People don't know that little carelessness
Can cause a big calamity.
So, stop what you're doing and step forward,
For your bright and new future.
Save water, save future,
Instead of spreading dirt, spread cleanliness.
Spread cleanliness, Spread happiness
Spread joy and mirth all around.

Ojasvi Khandelwal

Poem – 3
Christmas

All the months go past
But December is the last.
But December is the best
As Santa arrives as a guest
We hear the Christmas bells ring
And the melodious carols we sing
The pine tree spreads its glow
On the ground which is covered with snow
We distribute gifts all new
Hope all our wishes do come true!

Poem – 4

Flowers

Each passing day waiting for spring to return,

Patiently and eagerly for the winter snow to burn.

Glimmering in the sunshine how proud it glows.

Seen in almost every color our dear rose.

Facing towards the sun how beautiful it becomes,

Blooming soft golden petals with each drop of rain shower,

A bright, delicate and unique, our dear Sunflower.

Struggling through mud and dirt to grow,

But still spreading its stunning glow,

You have captured our heart and showed us,

To never give up in our lives oh dear lotus.

Orange as respect,

Yellow as happiness,

White as prosperity,

And pink as caring hearts,
Soft pearls of this flower are beautiful and fragment,
We all love you dearly, our dear lily.
Flowers like daisy, marigold and jasmine,
Are also unique in a special way,
Always brightening up our precious day,
Each passing day waiting for spring to return,
Patiently and eagerly for the winter snow to burn,
To enjoy these Awesome! Blossoms!

Ojasvi Khandelwal

Poem – 5

Summer

The fine Golden Sun glimmers and shines,
Spreading its bright and warm rays all over these days
Birds flying in the air
And toads floating on lily pads without a cave
My ice-cream is melting in this hot sunny day
I am trying to have it fast but it's dribbling away.
The sand is peach, the sea is blue,
A wonderful little beach, is waiting just for you,
When this season strikes,
The best thing to do is go on a hike,
Having a picnic with family and friends
Is the best way to have the time spent.
Behind these unusual activities,
What is the reason of this mysterious season?

Ojasvi Khandelwal

Poem – 6

Festivals

The auspicious time to set up idols
Waiting for the God's arrival
Cultures, regions and traditions
In various types of all the nation
All our festivals are our pride
Celebrated with joy far and wide
Because classical glory can never be compared
As it's enjoyed with lot of care
However, wherever, whenever time it comes
We celebrate it playing lazims and drum.
Rakhi, Navratri, Dussera, Diwali
We share love with our family

Beautiful Bharat

Eid, Christmas, lohri, onam
We always have the best fun
Holi, janmashtmi, chaturthi, sankranti
Always reciting pooja thankfully
Ramnavmi, mahashivratri, purnima, jayanti
Come let's celebrate you and me
Festivals are a symbol of unity
Celebrated with high diversity
Wearing beautiful attire on this occasion
Using our creation and innovation
We decorate our house keeping neat and clean
Keeping our surrounding always green
Distributing sweets all new
Hope our wishes do come true

Poem – 7

Chandrayaan – 3

Long through time awaited
Which left all Indians fascinated
The failure we will always regret
The success we can never forget
Moon our closest neighbor
Yet far from the earth's equator
Along the journey there will be trials
There will be agreements and denials
South pole region was still a mystery
The mission was at hold
But today it will be written in golden pages of history
The greatest gift ever unfold
Long through time awaited
Which left all Indians fascinated.
The failure we always regret
The success we can never forget

Also known as Chandrayaan -3
We showcased ISRO's technology
Before when countries laughed at us
We made them have an apology
Knowing our mission
Looking through our vision
Having a commission
Developing our position
A proud moment of 1400 million hearts
A great enjoyment, as we made a new start
Long through time awaited
Which left all Indians fascinated.
The failure we will always regret,
The success we can never forget.

Poem – 8
Wedding

Your happiness begins
on this bright wedding day
The beautiful couple twins
Have started their new way
Your families are dancing and singing
So don't pay attention on your phone ringing
Tasting and enjoying delicious food
According to the respective choice of our mood
Wearing shining unique Gold jewellery
That's delicate and sparks sparkly
Dressing up ourselves in a beautiful gown
Looking like kings and queens wearing a crown
So, go bloom
Dear bride and groom

Poem – 9

Bones

Without me you won't have any shape at all
Like a lump of clay or a punctured rubber ball.
I am long, I am short, I am big or small
You have me 206 in all
I am where your blood cells are made
I am what support you how you are weighed
Ribs are like a vest
You wear around your chest
Cranium is the main for your soft squishy brain
Mandible is in your inner mouth
Which is the largest and strongest throughout.
Scapula our shoulders blade
Sometimes shrinking to be afraid
Radius, ulna and humerous

Making our hand full of luminous
Carpals, metacarpals and phalanges
Helps us throughout difficult challenges
Fibula the lower leg, patella the knee cap
Hard to wreck or form a crap.
Though I am light, still on the fight,
Though I am strong, may not last very strong
Exercise, run, jump and dance
Maintain your posture and your stance
Have lots of minerals, calcium
Through dairy products
As this is what I instruct.

Poem – 10

God

In love we were created
All of the unique festivals celebrated.
In love we are sustained,
If we are spiritually attained.
The diverse universe created by you,
From all the problems you have come through.
The warmth of light
making the world so bright.
The magnificence of the sky,
For the birds to fly.
The calm and quite sea for the fishes to live,
On the land every tree which is more than enough to give.
Moon, stars, clouds and sun
Earth, water, fire and air

Beautiful Bharat

Everything is controlled in your hands
With lots of love and care.
You protect all the generous soul
All of us in your control.
If we are in trouble anywhere,
All we have to do is just recital a prayer.
Even if the world never saw your face,
We are fully aware of your grace.
The divine forms that you upholds,
Always supporting us in summer or cold.
Be Hindu or Christian, Muslim or Jain
If you call his precious name
God will reward you with love and fame
So be spiritually devoted
And this world will be more than expected.

Ojasvi Khandelwal

www.ingramcontent.com/pod-product-compliance
Lightning Source LLC
LaVergne TN
LVHW061628070526
838199LV00070B/6620